STACEY DEHASS

Celebrating SIMPLICITY
the starter kitchen

Celebrating Simplicity
© 2010 Stacey DeHass

All rights reserved. No portion of this book may be reproduced by any means, electronic or mechanical, including photocopying, recording, or by any information storage retrieval system, without permission of the copyright's owner, except for the inclusion of brief quotations for a review.

ISBN-13: 978-0-9819357-7-5

A Division of Liberty University Books
Lynchburg, VA

Cover & Interior Design:
Megan Johnson
Johnson2Design.com

To my wonderful and supportive Parents.

*For my Mom who taught me to treat everything I make like I am painting a picture, and make it beautiful.
Even a Peanut Butter and Jelly Sandwich!*

For my Dad who patiently taste tested all of my culinary creations. From omelets to campfire to every recipe in this book.

TABLE OF CONTENTS

Introduction — 1

Chapter 1: Equipment — 3

Bake Ware	3	Mixing Bowls	6
Sheet Trays	3	Graters	7
Iron Skillets	4	Electric Hand Mixer	7
Sauté Pans	4	Colander and Mesh Strainer	7
Stock Pots and Saucepans	5	Cutting Boards	7
Measuring Cups and Spoons	5	Pepper Grinder	8
Rubber Spatulas	5	Knife Drawer Insert	8
Wooden Spoons	5	Thermometer	9
Whisk	6	Kitchen Towels and Pot Holders	9
Vegetable Peeler	6	Storage Containers	9
Can Opener	6		

Chapter 2: Ingredients — 11

Kosher Salt	11	Garlic	15
Cayenne Pepper	11	Onions	15
Black Pepper	11	Olive Oil, Vegetable Oil	15
Flour	12	Vinegar	16
Sugar	12	Butter	16
Brown Sugar	12	Cheese	16
Honey	12	Milk	17
Baking Soda, Baking Powder	13	Cream	17
Vanilla	13	Eggs	17
Cinnamon	13	Chicken Stock	18
Potatoes	14	Frozen Vegetables and Fruit	18
Pasta	14	Ketchup, Mustard and Mayonnaise	19
Rice	14		

Chapter 3: How To — 21

Mise En Place	21	Knife Maintenance	27
Read a Recipe	23	Chop an Onion	30
Planning a Menu	24	Peel a Potato	32
Making a List	25	Roast Garlic	33
Measuring	25	Cleaning As You Go	35
Knife Skills	26		

Chapter 4: Recipes — 37

Starters — 37

Black Bean Soup	37
Chicken Noodle Soup	38
Potato Bacon Soup	40
Roasted Garlic Tomato Soup	41
Cheddar Biscuits	42
Grilled Garlic Bread	43
Roasted Chicken Pasta Salad	44

Mains — 47

Baked Rigatoni with Simple Meat Sauce	47
Meatloaf with Sweet Pepper Sauce	48
One Pot Chicken Pie	50
Quick Broiled Chicken Wings	52
Simple Roasted Chicken	54
Honey Lime Grilled Shrimp	56
Molasses Pork Tenderloin	58
Pasta with Ham and Peas	59
Simple Cheese Sauce	60
Zucchini and Chicken Lasagna	62

Sides — 64

Herb Roasted Sweet Potatoes	64
Pantry Potatoes	66
Roasted Asparagus	68
Home Style Cucumber Salad	69
Perfect Mashed Potatoes	70
Sautéed Green Beans	71

Desserts — 72

Cranberry Crumb Bread	72
Fruit Cobbler	73
Vanilla Butter Cookies	74
Quick Berry Cheesecake	76
Peach Blueberry Crisp	78
Apple Strudel	80

CELEBRATING SIMPLICITY

INTRODUCTION
The Starter Kitchen

WHETHER YOU ARE A STARVING college student, a nervous newlywed or a seasoned home cook, everyone needs a little help in the kitchen. It can be frightening to open the refrigerator and see nothing but bright lights and ketchup staring back at you. To study a recipe and not know how or where to start can be daunting. Sometimes it is as simple as learning how to put the chicken in the pan and the knife to the board. You don't have to be a trained chef, or even an obsessed foodie to know the ropes in your own kitchen.

The Starter Kitchen will break down the fundamentals of cooking with everything from how to stock your pantry to how to make the perfect dinner.

CHAPTER 1
Equipment

SPEND FIVE MINUTES IN ANY KITCHEN gadget store and your mind will go crazy wondering what you need and what you don't. The thought of apple corers, garlic peelers and hands free, smell free super quick onion choppers can be alluring. But, stop before you buy and think—can't all these things be done with the classic kitchen tools? I have created a list of kitchen tools that can get you through almost any recipe. This list will not only help you stock your cabinets, but also keep them from over flowing with gadgets years from now!

Bake Ware

A nice selection of bake ware, varying in size, shape and depth is necessary in any kitchen. I am drawn to ceramic dishes because I like how they look and they bake evenly. You can also use clear glassware, which has the added perk of being see-through, so you can check for doneness. I have no problem using metal baking dishes, but these options tend to be thinner, and could result in burnt edges. No matter what type of bake ware you choose, have fun with shapes like oval, square and rectangle.

Sheet Trays

Cookie sheets, sheet pans, or trays—whatever you choose to call them—are a must have. I keep it simple with a few different sizes of stainless steel or aluminum pans. It is good to have at least one coated, nonstick pan for things you are baking that might stick like cookies or biscuits. Remember that sheet pans see their fair share of wear, so you may not want to blow your kitchen budget on the most expensive brands.

CHAPTER 1: EQUIPMENT

Iron Skillets

There are so many fancy and expensive choices out there when it comes to cook ware. Where do you start? Copper? Stainless Steel? Non-Stick? When it comes to skillets, I keep it traditional: Cast Iron. My grandma and her grandma before her cooked with cast iron, so it is alright for me! Cast Iron is the ultimate in stove to oven to table cookware. It heats more evenly than the other pan options, and once it gets hot, it stays hot, making it perfect for pan searing. I keep a variety of skillet sizes handy, but you can choose the best size for you based on your own needs. The key to success with cast iron is that your pans are properly seasoned. If you are buying a new skillet, simply follow the directions for seasoning. Never wash them with soap, and coat with oil after each use. The best cast iron skillets, however, are the ones your grandma handed down to you, or you can readily find them at your local flea market.

Sauté Pans

In my experience cooking in other peoples kitchens, the one thing they lack most is a good set of sauté pans. I cannot count how many I have seen with the non-stick coating peeling off! When stocking your kitchen, step up and buy a good quality set of pans. I recommend one 8 inch sauté pan and one 12 inch sauté pan, one of which should be non-stick. With so many brands and styles out there it can be hard to choose what is right for you. Stick to a pan with a thick bottom and sturdy handle. Avoid using metal utensils on your non-stick pan, and if the coating starts to peel, it's time for a new pan.

Stock Pots and Saucepans

Much like sauté pans, it is good to purchase high-quality pots. I stock my cabinets with a large (10qt) and medium (6 qt) stock pot and one 3 quart saucepan. These are enough to get you through any recipe you will encounter. You should choose a brand with thick bottoms to prevent soups, stocks and sauces from sticking.

Measuring Cups and Spoons

There is no way to get through a recipe and not see lingo like cups, teaspoons and tablespoons. Unless you are a seasoned cook with an eye for measurements, you need measuring tools. A set of dry measuring cups in various sizes and a set of graduated measuring spoons are your best bet. It is also a good idea to have a "pitcher-like" liquid measuring cup. These are designed to make measuring liquids much simpler, since they leave a little space above the largest measurement, so the liquid doesn't spill.

Rubber Spatulas

Take it from me, the resident utensil "melter" in my household, it is important to have heat resistant rubber spatulas around. I find myself using these tools in many ways. They are a lifesaver when scraping dishes and trying to get every last mouthful out of the pan. They are perfect when folding egg whites into cream and they make a great tool for stirring things on the stove.

Wooden Spoons

Wooden spoons have been a kitchen essential for generations. This simple tool is a perfect all purpose utensil, even in a modern kitchen. They don't melt when used with high heats, and they don't scratch non-stick pans. The only worry with these spoons is that they burn when placed too close to the flame on certain stoves. You can purchase a cheap set of wooden spoons at any kitchen store, but remember not to wash them in the dish washer.

CHAPTER 1: EQUIPMENT

Whisk

Nothing can replace a good whisk when making a sauce or whipping cream. I use a simple metal whisk, with a comfortable handle. I have tried plastic whisks, but find they are simply not sturdy enough to withstand heavy mixing. I have also tried all of the different whisk styles, but always end up going back to the traditional whisk.

Vegetable Peeler

I have seen too many people cutting their hand trying to peel things with a paring knife, which is why I recommend a good old fashioned peeler. I use a peeler for things like potatoes, carrots and some cucumbers. I prefer the cheapest peelers on the market; they are about $1 and can be easily replaced if the blade dulls.

Can Opener

Hopefully your can opener's primary use is not for cracking open canned soup for dinner. Ideally you will use this tool to open canned favorites like petite diced tomatoes, black beans or even canned fruits. There is no need to buy the latest and greatest electric can opener, when a simple one—as shown—will do the trick.

Mixing Bowls

Mixing bowls are one of my most commonly used tools in the kitchen. I have a stackable set of both stainless steel and glass bowls. The sizes range from 2 gallon to 2 ounces and I never seem to have enough. I love to mix bread dough in the glass bowls, so I can watch the progress without lifting the cover. I use my stainless steel bowls when I am mixing something that needs to be chilled, like a berry sauce- things cool faster in steel bowls.

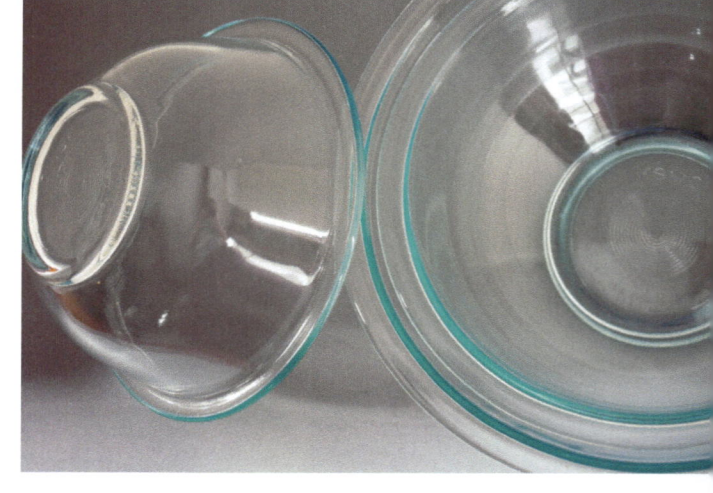

CELEBRATING SIMPLICITY

Graters

There seems to be a grater in every shape and size, for every variety of cheese, and in any radical color you can imagine. Cut through the clutter and buy two. A simple, four sided box grater is necessary for grating soft cheeses and even things like carrots and apples for salads. For hard cheeses, lemon zest and sometimes spices you should buy a "micro plane" grater. These graters have fine, super sharp blades and are "grate" for a more refined shred.

Electric Hand Mixer

Depending on how much you bake, you have two basic mixer choices. An electric hand mixer, or a large counter top stand mixer. If you bake one or two cakes a year, cookies every now and then and whipped cream occasionally—buy a hand mixer. If you are planning a Girl Scout bake sale, or have a husband with a sweet tooth- a stand mixer is right for you. They are pretty much interchangeable- all except for the price. I have both, and find I reach for the hand mixer most often.

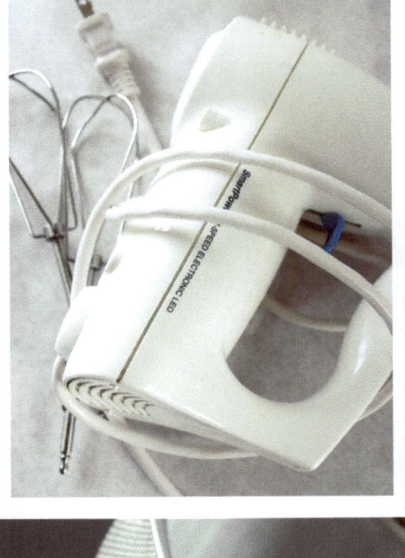

Colander and Mesh Strainer

A stainless steel colander is perfect for things like draining cooked pasta or potatoes or washing berries. You should purchase a quality stainless steel colander, because you will be pouring hot liquids through it most often. A fine mesh strainer with a handle is used for straining sauces or small items that would fall through the holes of a large colander. Both are important to have.

Cutting Boards

It is a good idea to keep at least one plastic cutting board and one wooden cutting board in your kitchen. Wood cutting boards are the best surface you can cut on to preserve the edge of your knife. They do, however, require special care. Never wash a wooden cutting board in the dishwasher, or leave it to soak in water. To clean, simply wipe with a soapy dish rag, then dry immediately. Some wooden cutting boards require oiling. To keep the grain moist and prevent cracking. Simply wipe the board down with a low grade olive oil once a month. Plastic cutting boards are useful and require very little maintenance. Use plastic boards to cut any raw meats and strong vegetables, like garlic, peppers and onions.

Pepper Grinder

Freshly ground black pepper has 10 times the flavor of that which is pre-ground and stored in the cabinet for ages. You can buy black peppercorns in bulk, and easily refill the grinders as needed. For my kitchen, I have two grinders: one that I keep by the stove, and one that has a salt shaker on top that I keep on the dinner table. Many pepper grinders are adjustable, so you can vary how fine you want them to grind.

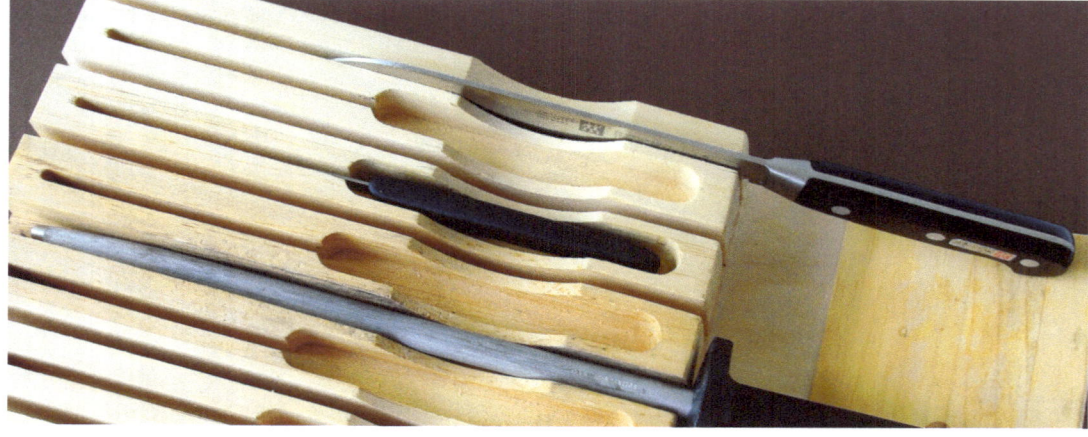

Knife Drawer Insert

As you will see in the how-to section of this book, proper knife storage is critical for the life of your knife. These drawer inserts store the knife edges safely in wood slots, keeping them organized and secure. Never store a knife in a cluttered utensil drawer—this not only dulls the edge, but can also be dangerous. No one wants to cut themselves on a hidden knife! You can also buy a wooden storage block for your knifes, but I prefer the drawer version, as it can be tucked out of the way, leaving more counter space.

CELEBRATING SIMPLICITY

Thermometer

There is so much confusion as to how to tell when meat, especially chicken, is fully cooked. The only tried and true way to know for sure is to check the temperature. A simple stem thermometer is all you need. They are very accurate and easy to read. For more on how to use a thermometer, see the "how to" section of this book.

Kitchen Towels and Pot Holders

Simple, plain towels are irreplaceable in the kitchen. No one wants to use their decorative towels for cleaning up a mess. When purchasing kitchen towels, look for ones that are made from thick terry cloth, as they are much more absorbent. It is also a good idea to have a set of thick pot holders near your oven. Most of the time a folded kitchen towel works for removing things from the oven, but if they are wet you will burn your hand. To be on the safe side, use pot holders.

Storage Containers

Last… but not least! Plastic storage containers are a necessary evil in a well stocked kitchen. No matter how hard we try not to, we will always have leftovers. The one thing we can prevent, however, is creating plastic ware pile up. In my pantry I limit myself to 10-20 storage containers of various sizes. It is not necessary to have any more than that. The key to handling leftovers gracefully is dating food items as they go into the refrigerator. A simple piece of masking tape and a marker will do the trick. Leftovers can be used for up to 7 days. To be on the safe side, however, I have a five day rule for most ultra perishable items.

CHAPTER 1: EQUIPMENT

CHAPTER 2
Ingredients

ALL OF THE KITCHEN GADGETS money can buy are no help without the proper ingredients. Knowing what to buy, how to choose it, how to store it and how to use it can be tough. The refrigerator can turn into a place where food goes to die. I, myself, have been accused of using my refrigerator as a home for science projects! The pantry can become an area to store mountains of Tupperware and canned soup. Everyone wants to be more organized, but where to start? I have come up with my Top 20(ish) Ingredients that every cook should stock in their kitchen. By keeping these staples on hand you have the basics of endless recipes at your fingertips.

Kosher Salt, Cayenne Pepper, Black Pepper

I call this my trilogy of seasonings. You could put me in the middle of the woods with an iron skillet, a match and these three ingredients and I could throw together a gourmet meal. So many cooks think that loading a dish with exotic spices and seasonings is the way to a solid recipe. I have found that starting with good quality ingredients and bringing out their natural flavor saves me from having to cover up with spices galore.

I use kosher salt exclusively in my kitchen. A dinner guest at my house will have to search the cupboards to find a salt shaker of iodized table salt. I love kosher salt for many reasons. The course texture makes it easier to pinch and regulate the amount of salt you put in a recipe. The flavor is smooth, and lacks the "chemical" taste that iodized salt is known to have. When using kosher salt, take the time to bring out the flavors of the dish, then add salt by the pinch. Simmer, then taste, as the flavors take some time to marry. If you find the taste is lacking, add another pinch, simmer and taste again.

There is always a pepper grinder by my stove, filled to the brim with whole peppercorns. The flavor of pepper is essential with most savory recipes, and when it is freshly cracked, the effect is far superior. If a recipe is seasoned well and tasted before it is served, no one should ever have to douse the dish in salt and pepper.

Have you ever tasted a recipe and thought... this needs something? Most often that something is just a little kick. I use cayenne pepper in many different applications, to simply round out the flavor of a recipe. If you have a cream sauce for instance, add just a pinch of cayenne pepper. This is not to add spice, but it is to lift the rich flavors off of your tongue and create balance in the recipe.

Flour

All purpose flour is a must in any pantry. Flour has many uses, from baking a cake to breading chicken or to thicken the perfect gravy. Buy a five pound bag of your favorite brand of all purpose flour and store it in an airtight container in your pantry. It is also good to buy a small, two pound bag of self rising flour. This specialty flour is a common ingredient in many baked goods.

Sugar

Simple fine white sugar belongs in everyone's kitchen. It is essential in baking everything from bread to pie crust to a complicated layer cake. Sugar also has a place on the savory side of the kitchen. Green beans are nothing without a dash of sugar, tomato sauce needs sugar to polish the flavor, and let's not forget good old southern sweet tea!

Brown Sugar

What most people don't know about brown sugar is that it is simply white sugar combined with molasses. Brown sugar is usually found in two types—light or dark. I stock light brown sugar in my pantry; it has the rich flavor of molasses, but it is not as intense as the dark version. Brown sugar is great in all sorts of dishes, from caramel to fruit crisps to barbeque sauces. Be sure to store brown sugar in an airtight container or sealed bag, or it will become hard as a rock!

Honey

Honey is perhaps one of the oldest and most natural sweeteners that you can use. Although it is a bit pricey, it packs a powerful, concentrated flavor and is worth every penny. Honey is my primary source of sweetness in my cooking or baking. It should be stored in a cool dark place for up to one year. If you find that your honey has begun to crystallize (it will look grainy and white) simply pop the opened container in the microwave for about thirty seconds.

CELEBRATING SIMPLICITY

Baking Soda and Baking Powder

You will hardly ever find a baked item like cookies, cakes or biscuits that doesn't use baking soda and/or baking powder. While both are known as chemical leaveners that make a baked good rise, they are often used together.

Vanilla

A small bottle of pure vanilla extract will see you through nearly any dessert recipe. Pure vanilla extract is the only way to go, but it can be rather expensive. Don't skimp! Buy the real thing because imitation vanilla tends to have a "chemical" taste.

Cinnamon

Ground cinnamon appears in many of my sweet dessert recipes. A dash here and there adds a brilliantly subtle flavor that I love. A small container will get you through many dessert recipes, since cinnamon is usually not used in large quantities.

CHAPTER 2: INGREDIENTS

Potatoes

I try to pair a starch with every meal. For me, this is usually found in the form of pasta, rice or some sort of potato. I always keep a variety of potatoes in my pantry, like Yukon gold, Red Skins or a simple Idaho. Store the potatoes in a basket in the coolest darkest section of your pantry. This will stave off the sprouts for a bit longer. With potatoes always on hand you have a quick solution to any last minute meal planning.

Pasta

Pasta is a mainstay in my pantry. Just when you think you have nothing to eat, you can make many great meals with pasta. I always keep a large variety of pasta in the pantry, like some different cuts of long pasta, such as spaghetti, linguine or fettuccine. These can be great if I want to make a meal out of them, or simply serve them seasoned alongside a great piece of fish. I also keep some small cuts, such as macaroni, rotini, or farfalle (bow tie) available. I love a quick meal with chicken, peas and rotini — or the ever popular macaroni and cheese in a pinch. There are so many different shapes and sizes of pasta; have fun with it and try them all!

Rice

Rice is a versatile grain that can be found in many different forms. The most common in my pantry are long grain white, brown and short grain white. Long grain rice is just that- a longer, thin grain. The shape and texture makes this type perfectly light and fluffy when cooked. On the other hand a short grain rice will create a sticky end result. Long grain is great for stir fries and simple sides. Short grain is best when made into a risotto. I also have brown rice on hand. The only difference between this and the white varieties is brown rice has the shell on each grain. This difference means it will take much longer to cook, and has a courser texture. The flavor is so rich, though and can just be served with a bit of butter and salt.

Garlic

Garlic can be an amazing and flavorful addition to many savory recipes. The key is knowing when to stop. There is a fine line between the perfect amount of garlic and going horribly overboard. You can buy garlic by the bulb in your grocery store, and store it in a cool dry area of your pantry. The best way to use garlic in a recipe is by roasting it. This simple process brings out the garlic's natural sweetness and can be used just like raw garlic in any recipe. {refer to How to Roast Garlic on page 33}

Onions

Sweet yellow onions are a necessity for any pantry. Although onions have a bad reputation, and are disliked by many, when prepared correctly they can be really great. When purchasing onions, be sure to buy sweet Vidalia onions, or at least yellow onions. White or Purple onions have an extremely harsh flavor. Store onions in a cool dry section of your pantry; some onions can be kept for a few months. If you notice your onions starting to sprout (growing a green stem), discard them and buy fresh.

Olive Oil and Vegetable Oil

Oils are essential in many different forms of cooking. They are used in anything from frying, to cake baking, to making salad dressings. I always have two varieties of oil in my pantry. I use a simple olive oil, rather than extra virgin. I prefer the taste of a mid level olive oil over extra virgin oil (as extra virgin tends to be overpowering). I also buy vegetable oil. This oil is best when cooking at high temperatures—for instance, when you are frying.

Vinegar

Vinegar can be used for so much more than sprinkling it on your French fries or turnip greens! It is good to keep apple cider vinegar for recipes such as barbeque sauces and marinades. I love balsamic vinegar because it has a rich, sweet flavor that is good for many uses. A simple white wine vinegar comes in handy when you need just a touch of tartness, without the color. In many of my recipes I use just a dash of vinegar to round out the flavor. Never ever use distilled white vinegar for cooking. This vinegar variety is over processed and has a harsh flavor—it is only good for cleaning!

Butter

Ah! Butter! Quite possibly my favorite of all ingredients. I would like to say that my cooking is low fat, but nearly all of my recipes call for butter. Whether I am pan frying something, finishing a sauce or making pie crust- butter is my go-to. Butter is one of the most natural fats you can use, and when eaten in moderation—it simply cannot be bad for you. Clear your refrigerator of any scary substitutes—because butter is back in style—and butter is best!

Cheese

Whether you are making a sandwich or having a quick snack, cheese is a must-have for your refrigerator. I try to keep a wide variety of cheeses, such as Swiss, cheddar and parmesan. Unless you are a heavy cheese eater, buy cheese in smaller quantities, so it doesn't go to waste if it molds. Most cheeses, however, can be salvaged if they mold. Simply shave off the mold and discard it.

CELEBRATING SIMPLICITY

Milk

Simple, whole cow's milk is great for so much more than just drinking, dousing cereal and dunking cookies! Milk is a mainstay in many dessert recipes and also makes an appearance in savory cooking. If your household is not made up of milk drinkers and cereal eaters, simply keep a half gallon in the refrigerator for cooking.

Cream

Cream can be a scary ingredient in a recipe. I will admit to making recipes that call for a somewhat large amount of cream. However, cream can be used sparingly and can fit into any healthy diet plan. When I am looking for a rich cream flavor without the fat, I use a simple trick. Substitute the cream in any recipe with whole milk. Then, just add a tablespoon of cream to achieve the richness you want.

Eggs

Even if you are not a fan of a good old fried egg for breakfast, you must keep a carton of eggs in your refrigerator. Eggs have a very long shelf life, and are an ingredient in many recipes, especially baked goods. When cracking eggs, always tap the egg on a flat surface, as opposed the edge of a bowl, this keeps unwanted shell pieces from getting into the egg. Also, crack each egg needed in the recipe into a small bowl so you can check for shells and or any spoilage or discoloration. One bad egg, or shell piece can bring down a whole recipe.

CHAPTER 2: INGREDIENTS

Chicken Stock

If you are a fan of soups, gravies or sauces—who isn't—chicken stock has a place in your refrigerator. I buy a good quality chicken base, which is simply chicken stock that has been reduced to a paste. This way I can just add water and have the perfect amount of stock for my recipe. You can also buy chicken stock in the soup isle of your grocery store. Look for one that is labeled "stock"—not "broth". Stock is made from simmering chicken bones and parts, giving it a full and rich flavor. Broth is generally made from simmered meat, leaving the flavor a bit lacking. I use chicken stock in many sauces, even for pork dishes, because the flavor is subtle and blends well. If you are making a beef recipe, however, grab some beef stock while you are at the grocery store.

Frozen Vegetables and Fruit

Nowadays so many people have their freezer jam packed full of ice cream bars and readymade meals. Throw out the pre-made quickie meals and replace them with wholesome frozen vegetables and fruit. My freezer is always stocked with frozen peas, green beans and sweet corn. Having these items on hand is a good way to keep vegetables in your diet, even when you haven't been to the grocery in a while. I also love frozen fruit such as peaches, cherries and various berries. These fruits, just like vegetables, are frozen in the peak of their season, making them the sweetest and best they can be- unless you eat them fresh, of course. Frozen fruits can be substituted for fresh in almost any recipe—especially cobblers and crisps.

Ketchup, Mustard and Mayonnaise

If you are planning to have a backyard barbeque, you should have these condiments for obvious reasons. But they are useful for so much more than burger toppings. They also seem to last forever in your refrigerator! All of these condiments can be used in a wide range of sauces such as barbeque sauce, salad dressing and even marinades. Keep whatever brand your family likes on hand.

CHAPTER 3
How To

Mise En Place (MEEZ-ahn-plahs)

The concept of organized cooking hit me like a brick at a very young age. My parents were advocates of working clean, cleaning as you go and most of all—working smart. It wasn't until my first years of culinary school that I learned a phrase that encompassed it all. Mise en place. Finally. A fancy French word for something I had known all along.

Technically speaking Mise en Place means "Everything in its place". This spans from everything to salt and pepper, to spatulas and pans.

Successful Mise en Place begins with these easy steps:

Read the Recipe: (please see: how to read a recipe) Once you have read through and determined that you have all the ingredients and equipment necessary to make the dish, you are almost ready to begin.

Mental Mise en Place: This is a term that I use widely. When I am prepping important dishes, I sometimes go so far as to close my eyes and wave my arms wildly in a sautéing motion. Although that is extreme, you should walk through each step of the recipe in your head before even picking up a knife. This step will help you manage your time wisely.

Gather: I start by getting each piece of equipment I need to tackle the dish. If there is any cutting or chopping involved, prepare your cutting board station. This simply means placing a damp towel beneath your board to keep it from slipping, then grabbing any knife you might use along the way. Also obtain the pots, pans, utensils, or measuring cups you will need.

Next, grab the ingredients. It is helpful to manage your steps and make as few trips as possible to the pantry, refrigerator or spice cabinet.

Pre-Prep: At this stage, do any prep work necessary before the actual cooking begins. For example, chop the vegetables, measure the chicken stock, start the water boiling, preheat the oven. This will save you a world of frustration.

Begin: Now, after carefully reading the steps in your recipe, begin cooking. It is at this stage that most people get flustered. It is their natural tendency to poke, prod, and stir… or the dreaded opening of the oven to take a peek! If your recipe says to stir constantly, do so. If something is sautéing at high heat, give it a shake or two now and then. If something is supposed to bake for twenty minutes, shut the door and walk away. You will lose so much heat—and cooking time—by checking over and over. It is at this stage in the game that you must begin to multi task. If you are preparing a meal, and not just one recipe, work on another dish. If you are not making any other recipe, clean up the dishes. Gather your service ware. Set the table. Grab a cocktail. Anything but frantically check the oven! Ever heard the expression… a watched pot never boils? Live by that.

The whole concept of *Mise en Place* can seem overwhelming. But, really, each step is simple and once you force yourself to do it, it will become second nature to you. Your food will turn out better, because you are organized instead of frantic. Your kitchen will be cleaner, because you aren't dirtying unnecessary dishes. Therefore, you will be happier in the kitchen!

How to Read a Recipe

Most people I know judge a recipe not by how great it sounds, or what they have in their pantry… but by how long it is, and how complicated it looks. I am one of those people! If a recipe has too many ingredients, steps or long procedures, I steer clear. A simple way to solve this problem is to learn how to read a recipe- how to attack it!

BAKED RIGATONI WITH SIMPLE MEAT SAUCE

1 lb Ground Beef

1 16 oz Petite Dice Tomatoes, with juice

1 pt Grape Tomatoes, whole

Salt and Pepper to taste

2 tsp Olive Oil

1 tsp Balsamic Vinegar

4 quarts Water

1 Tbsp Kosher Salt

½ lb Uncooked Rigatoni Pasta

1 cup Mozzarella Cheese, grated

Cook ground beef over medium heat in a medium saucepan, or tall sided sauté pan. Drain grease when meat is cooked. Stir in canned tomatoes and simmer over medium heat, uncovered, for ½ hour. Season to taste and add olive oil and vinegar.

While the sauce is simmering bring 4 quarts of water and kosher salt to a boil. Cook pasta according to package instructions. Drain pasta and rinse with cool running water.

Toss pasta with sauce and place into a 9x13. Top with grated cheese.

Bake pasta at 375 degrees for about 15 minutes, until the cheese is melted and the sauce is bubbly.

Start by reading the entire recipe through. When scanning the ingredients ask yourself a few questions:

Do I have all of the ingredients? If not choose another recipe, or put the items on your grocery list for later.

Is there anything in this recipe my family doesn't like… what can I substitute?

Start your Mise En Place by gathering all of the ingredients and getting ready for preparation.

CHAPTER 3: HOW TO

Planning a Menu

Why wait until you feel that familiar growl of your stomach to plan what you are going to eat for dinner. Planning a weekly menu is as easy as choosing what to wear, and should become your habit. Here are a few simple tips to make menu planning fun and easy...

Make the Time: Set aside time in your week to sit down with your family and jot down some menu ideas. A leisurely Sunday Afternoon is a perfect time to discuss what your eaters are hungry for. Once you have planned a good menu, you can make a quick grocery list and be good to go. Your family will love knowing what is for dinner ahead of time, and before you know it menu planning will become routine.

Discuss Your Schedules: Any recipe can sound tasty and easy when you are planning your menu. An important thing to keep in mind is your family's schedule for the upcoming week. If you have a busy night coming up, choose a recipe that can be made ahead, or quickly put together. If you have some spare time, try something new that might challenge you.

Remember Your Proteins: Proteins always tend to be the center of a meal. Keep in mind the meats that your family likes and try to cycle each one into your meal plan. My family tends to eat beef, pork, chicken and the occasional fish and seafood. Knowing what your family likes, and using the different varieties and cuts makes menu planning a snap. For instance, with chicken, don't just buy chicken breasts. From one week to the next you can try chicken legs, thighs, wings or even a whole chicken.

Get Inspired: The same old thing week in and week out can get boring. A good way to spark some ideas is to pick up some cooking magazines, or cookbooks with pictures. This will help give everyone some inspiration, but keep a pen and paper handy; their ideas might keep you writing!

Leave a Little Extra: When you are planning dinner... don't forget lunch! Make note of things that are easily reheated, like soups or casseroles. Also, try revamping leftovers for exciting next day lunches. If you have sautéed green beans for dinner, eat them cold the next day with your favorite salad dressing. If you roasted a chicken and have leftover- pick the meat from the bone and make Roasted Chicken Pasta Salad for lunch.

Budget: Glance over the grocery advertisements in your local paper. There you can find great deals and work them into your weekly meal plan. This is also a good way to know what veggies are in season, because they go on sale when they are most plentiful.

Keep Track: Every little girl has tried to keep a diary once or twice in her life. I failed at this practice miserably until I started keeping a food diary. Each night that I cook, I record the recipes that I used, and how it went over. This is a great way to remember what recipes your family likes or dislikes. Grab the journal when you are planning your menu and flip through old entrees -- that is sure to make your family crave an old favorite.

Making a List

Now that you have a masterfully planned menu, the next step is making a grocery list. It is important to be as thorough as possible, so you don't spend your week running back and forth to the store- or to your neighbors for a cup of sugar!

Start by reading through your recipes and making note of what you have on hand. Having staple items in your pantry, fridge and freezer save time and money when you hit the store.

Check the items that you don't keep at home and write them down. It is helpful to record quantities on your list, so you know how much you need when you are at the store.

Scan the house for extra items you might need on the list. Nowadays grocery stores are SUPER markets and you can get all you need in one big trip. This will save you time and money in the long run.

Measuring

It seems one of the most complicated things about understanding a recipe is reading the measurements. What is this mysterious other language? I am among the majority and can say that I have confused teaspoon for tablespoon a time or two. The worst was in a life or death biscuit cook off when I was about 12 years old! Those were some salty biscuits! (I lost.)

To help you understand the wild world of measurements and abbreviations, I have broken the terms in this book down to the basics. After this crash course you should feel well prepared—and bilingual!

CHAPTER 3: HOW TO

Tsp: Teaspoon

Tbsp: Tablespoon

Pinch: The amount achieved when the ingredient is "pinched" between your thumb and index finger.

To Taste: This is the best way to measure things like salt and pepper, as everyone's tastes vary.

> *How to season to taste? Seasoning to taste comes with practice, and requires you to really use your taste buds. If the recipe calls for salt and pepper to taste, add a pinch of each, then continue cooking for about one minute before you taste. This allows the flavor to set in. If you are satisfied with the flavor, you are good to go. If not, season again and repeat. Be careful not to add too much at one time, as a little goes a long way!*

Cups: If the recipe call for dry ingredients, use a dry measuring cup, if it calls for a liquid use a liquid measuring cup.

Knife Skills

An entire chapter of this book—or even an entire book—could be dedicated to knives. Rather than delving into every detail of the knife, I want to feed you the need-to-know information. What do you need to know to pick up a knife and get to work?

Perhaps one of the most popular kitchen accessories on the planet is a knife block. The reality of these sets is they are packed with knives, of every shape and size that you never use. Sets of knives tend to be expensive, so rather than biting the bullet for 10 or 12 knives that will collect dust, stick to the essentials.

7 inch Chef's Knife or Santoku: Having a high quality large knife and knowing how to use it will change the way you cook. A 7-inch stainless steel chef's knife should cost anywhere from $60-$100. If you tend to cook a lot, splurge a bit more for the better knife. The beauty of these knives is that they last forever and are generally a one-time purchase. There are two main choices when choosing an all-purpose knife: the traditional chef's knife or the santoku knife: santokus are a Japanese design that is growing in popularity. I prefer them because the rounded top and slightly curved blade make chopping a breeze.

5 inch Boning Knife: Even if you don't see yourself cutting up a chicken anytime soon, it is still good to have a boning knife. The flexible blade makes this knife wonderfully all purpose. As with any knife that you buy make sure that it is fully forged. This means that the steel of the blade continues all the way through the handle of the knife, making it more durable and balanced. If the knife packaging does not say forged, chances are it is not, since it is a feature to brag about. A boning knife of good quality should cost $40-$70.

Paring Knives: Although many cooks use these small knives for anything from peeling an apple to dicing a potato, they are best suited for small jobs. A straight edge paring knife and a curved blade knife(called tourne or birds beak) are all you need. I prefer cheaper paring knives, as they tend to be made of a simple light weight plastic and acceptable stainless steel. This way they are easy to grip, and don't weigh your hands down when you're working. These knives normally run anywhere from $10-$15 dollars.

Knife Maintenance

Now that you are well stocked with high quality knives, it is important to know how to maintain them.

Storage: To store your knives, you can purchase a wooden drawer insert. The inserts have slots for the knives that keep the knife edges from wear. A run-of-the-mill insert with space for 6-8 large knives and 4-6 small ones only costs about $20-$30.

Sharpening: It has been said that a dull knife is more dangerous than a sharp one. I know this from true life experience—you apply more pressure than necessary when trying to cut with a dull knife—hence more pressure is applied when cutting yourself! Ouch! Regularly using a steel (as shown in the picture) is the easiest way to maintain the sharpness of your knives.

A steel is used to hone the edge of your knife, not sharpen or create a new edge. When cutting, the thin metal of the knife blade weakens and curls; this is called a bur. Most quality steels are magnetic and should be used between each time you use your knife; this will knock off the "bur" and maintain your edge. It is important to get your knife professionally sharpened every few months, depending on how often you use it.

The best way to learn to use your steel is to place the pointed tip on a sturdy surface. Securely hold the handle with your left hand. Now, hold the handle of the knife firmly in your right hand. Hold the back of the knife at a 20 degree angle against the steel. While maintaining a 20 degree angle, apply some pressure and slide the knife from back to tip down the steel (as shown). It is important to mirror this step on both sides of the blade. Repeat this 6-10 times on each side. Before cutting, carefully wipe the blade of your knife with a damp rag, to remove any metal fragments.

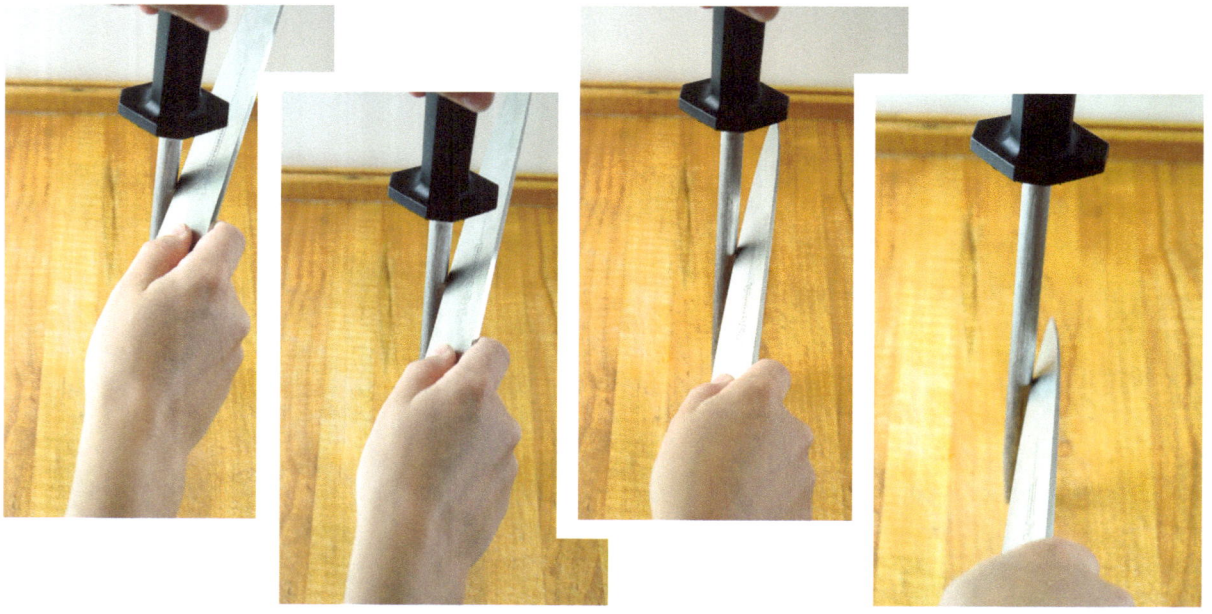

Knife Usage: For some cooks, using a big knife can be intimidating, as it should be! No matter how confident I am in my knife skills, I am still aware of what could happen if I make a simple mistake.

It is important to know the proper way to hold a knife, so you can be well on your way to success. A good quality chef's knife is made to be balanced, so when it is in your hands it won't weigh you down.

1. Do not hold your knife as shown in this picture. By gripping the very end of the handle you are losing any balance or control you have with the knife.

2. Although it may look fancy, keep your pointer finger off of the top of the knife. Once again, this throws of your balance, and makes you work harder than necessary.

3. The proper, and safest way to hold a knife is by gripping it with your thumb and pointer finger on the blade. Just like choking up on a baseball bat to give yourself leverage to swing. When

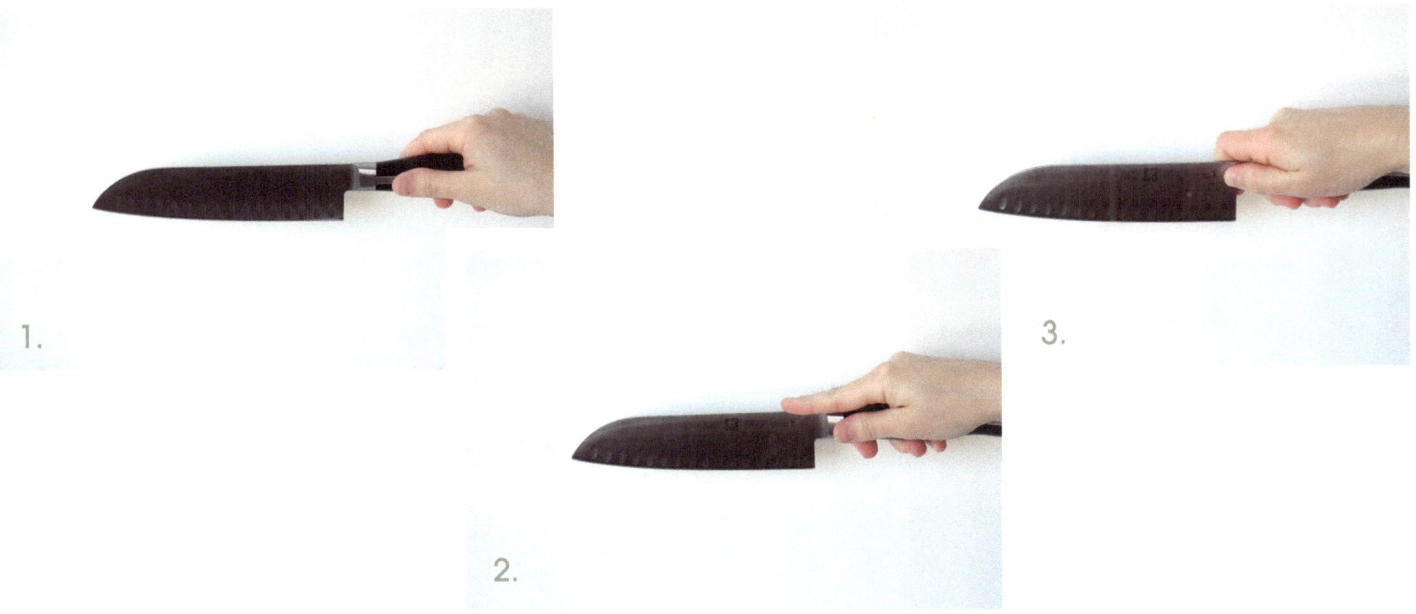

using this grip, make sure to keep your other fingers tucked away. This method will allow you to hold the knife firmly, and control each movement gracefully.

The shape of the blade on a chef's knife is slightly curved, and is meant to be rocked back and forth when cutting. To do this, start by placing your left hand (if you are right hand dominant) on the item you are cutting as shown. Make a flat edge from your second knuckle to yo ur fingernail. When you get really good the knife should touch this edge, and it will become a guide when cutting. For now, just use this hand to hold the item you are cutting in place, and keep your fingers out of the way, as shown. Begin cutting with the point of the knife on the board, then roll the knife so that the entire blade- front to back- makes contact with the board. You should never lift the tip of the knife from the board completely. This will result in a loud chop-chop-chop noise that is really just a waste of energy, and will dull your knife.

CHAPTER 3: HOW TO

How to Chop an Onion

Cutting Onions: One of the most dreaded procedures in the kitchen. From the burning eyes to complicated techniques, onion chopping is just a pain. Through the years I have learned that I can't just stop using onions all together, so I have fine tuned my chopping method.

Start by removing both the root end and the stem end.

Then slice the onion in half, from top to bottom. Then peel away the papery skin.

The key to this onion cutting technique is following the natural lines on the onion. As you can see, there are horizontal and vertical lines. These will be your guidelines.

Lay one of the onion halves on the flat side. Slice pieces across the wide part on the onion, according to how big you want your final result to be. Be sure to keep the slices together.

Rotate the onion one quarter turn. Notice the lines going horizontally across the onion. Simply follow the lines with your knife, change the angle of your knife as you follow the lines.

Continue these steps on the other half of the onion, and the result will be perfect and uniform dices, without the hassle!

CHAPTER 3: HOW TO

How to Peel a Potato

Sometimes the simplest things can be overcomplicated. Peeling a potato should be as quick and easy as boiling water. So why is it that when you are staring at a five pound bag of potatoes, you are intimidated? Follow these instructions and soon you'll be peeling potatoes like a sailor!

Knowing how to peel a potato with a paring knife is important. But, for most people, that results in crazy amounts of waste and bloody fingers. Using a sharp vegetable peeler gets the job done, and drastically reduces waste. When using a veggie peeler, your first reaction is to make quick, choppy little cuts.

Instead, start by cutting each end of the potato.

Hold the peeler just like you would a paring knife, and make long, smooth strokes toward you. Guide your cuts by resting your thumb on the potato for balance. Rotate the potato until all of the skin is removed.

CELEBRATING SIMPLICITY

How to Roast Garlic

It is common for folks to say that they don't like garlic. Garlic gives me heartburn. Garlic gives me bad breath. Perhaps all of that can be true in the kitchen of a garlic-loving Italian, but there is a better way to do garlic. Straight off the bulb the flavor of garlic can be harsh and hot tasting. One technique I use to reduce the severity of garlic is roasting it. This simple process brings out the natural sweetness and makes the overall flavor smooth and tasty.

Begin by cutting the top end off of a whole bulb of garlic.

This should expose all of the wonderful little cloves of garlic, while keeping them tightly in their skins.

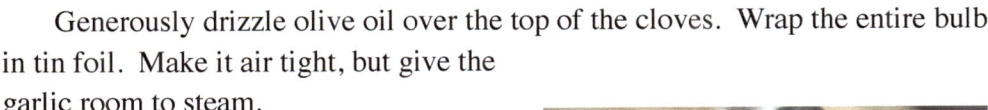

Generously drizzle olive oil over the top of the cloves. Wrap the entire bulb in tin foil. Make it air tight, but give the garlic room to steam.

Place foil packet in a 325 degree oven for 2-3 hours. Your entire kitchen will soon start to smell like heaven! After roasting, be careful when removing the bulb from the foil; there is a lot of hot steam trapped in that packet. Once roasted, each clove of garlic can be squeezed from its shell, and the result is sticky sweet, robust flavored garlic.

I like to roast a few bulbs at a time. They can be stored in the refrigerator for up to 7 days and make great additions to many recipes

Cleaning as You Go

I have asked many people why they don't like to cook. The overwhelming response has been… because they don't like to clean up! I can see how this would be a problem if you leave everything to the end and are exhausted by the effort. I would like to believe that between my older sister, younger brother and me, I was assigned "dish duty" more than anyone as a child. My sister was mysteriously ellusive at dish time, and my brother always had a perfectly timed trip to the bathroom. So that left me. The sad middle child and dish master. As I got older, I refined the art. I learned that what my Dad said was true: "If you don't make the mess, you won't have to clean it up!"

Cleaning as you go is simple. If you dirty a dish, wash it right away. Part of my *Mise en Place* anytime I am in the kitchen is to fill the sink with soapy water and clear the dish rack of any clean dishes. This way you are ready to roll in the dishwashing department.

During the steps of your cooking, wipe up the messes you make. Keep the counters clean and put things away when you are done using them. By the time your meal or recipe is nearing completion, your clean up should be as well.

Many people these days have dishwashers, but I find they are no good for washing large pots and pans. Before the era of dishwashers, my great-grandmother would clean up all of the pots and pans before she served the meal. I have only just begun this technique, and have found great success with it. Transfer the meal onto serving dishes, or individual plates, depending on what it is. Then, with your pre-drawn sink of water, quickly wash each pot and pan. This is helpful for many reasons. You can attack the problem dishes before the food has dried onto them. It is also nice to get up from the dinner table and only have the easy stuff like plates to wash. If you have a handy helper in the kitchen (like a middle child!), have them ready to wash each pan as you plate the meal. This makes the task even easier.

CHAPTER 3: HOW TO

CHAPTER 4
Recipes

STARTERS

Black Bean Soup

This recipe will serve 4-6 people and makes a great carry in dish to a party!

This black bean soup is a wonderfully quick soup to make, and is good for lunch or dinner. Be sure not to miss the garnish of sour cream… it is the best part!

1 Tbsp Olive Oil

½ Small Onion

½ Cup Red Peppers

½ Cup Sweet Corn, frozen

¾ Cup Chicken Stock

2 Cans Black Beans, with juice

Salt and Pepper to taste

¼ Tsp Chili Sauce

2 Tbsp Butter

4 Tbsp Sour Cream

First, chop the pepper and onion in ¼ inch dices. In a medium stock pot, over medium heat, heat oil. When oil is hot add onions and sauté for 5-10 minutes on low. You want the onions to get a deep caramel color, so they are sweet, not harsh. Stir frequently.

Turn heat to medium and add peppers. Sauté for 2 minutes. Add the corn and sauté for one more minute.

Add chicken stock and beans, turn heat to high and bring to a boil. Boil for 4-5 minutes. Add butter and chili sauce. Season to taste.

Serve with a tablespoon of sour cream on each portion. Optional: Garnish with chopped green onions.

Chicken Noodle Soup

Serves 4-6 comfortably…and you can even have leftovers!

On a cold day or a rainy evening, nothing beats a big pot of chicken noodle soup! This recipe is the basic, no frills version and the steps may seem like a lot, but each one is simple. Next time you have a craving for Chicken Noodle Soup, take the time to make this recipe!

6 Quarts Water

1, 3 lb Chicken

2 Carrots

½ Sweet Onion

2 Stalks Celery

3 Cloves Garlic

¾ Cup Sweet Onion, small dice

¼ Cup Celery, small dice

¾ Cup Carrots, small dice

1 ½ Cup Potatoes, small dice

2 Tbsp Butter

¼ Cup Flour

½ Cup Sweet Corn

½ Cup Lima Beans

½ Cup Green Beans

3 Cups Wide Egg Noodles

Place one whole chicken, purchased in quarters, in a large 8 quart stock pot.

Chop carrots, celery and onion into large pieces. Peel 3 cloves of garlic. Place veggies in stock pot with chicken and cover with 6 quarts water.

Allow this mixture to simmer, over low heat, for 2-3 hours. Do not boil. Boiling will cause the stock to become cloudy. After 3 hours, remove chicken pieces from the stock and place on a plate to cool. Strain stock through a fine mesh strainer into a large bowl. Reserve stock for later.

In the same stock pot that the stock was simmered in, melt butter and add diced vegetables.

CELEBRATING SIMPLICITY

Allow vegetables to cook over medium heat, stirring frequently, for 5 minutes. Turn heat to low and add flour. Cook for 1 minute while stirring. Carefully pour chicken stock into the vegetable flour mixture, then add corn, lima beans and green beans. These vegetables can be frozen or fresh, depending on the season. You can also add other vegetables that you like such as peas, bell peppers or sweet potatoes. Turn heat to high and bring to a boil. Once boiling, add egg noodles. Cook the noodles according to the time on the package instructions.

In the meantime, while you are waiting for the stock and vegetables to boil, pick the chicken from the bones using your hands. Discard any bones or fat, and be careful not to miss any small bone pieces. Break chicken into bite size pieces.

Once the noodles are cooked, stir the chicken into the soup and season to taste. You should add the seasoning gradually, simmer, then taste again. This soup is great served right away, or- as with most soups—is wonderful the next day!

Potato Bacon Soup with Smoked Cheddar

Serves 4-6

Whether it is a cold winter day or a dreary spring evening, potato soup makes a wonderfully hearty meal. This recipe is my basic recipe, but I love to add other things I have on hand. Don't be afraid to experiment. Try corn, red peppers, mushrooms or even broccoli. The base of this soup is the base to about any cream soup you can think of—so have fun with it.

- 8-10 Slices Bacon, diced
- ¾ Cup Flour
- 6 Cups Chicken Stock
- 3 Cups Potatoes, diced
- 2 Cups Milk
- 1 ½ Cup Smoked Cheddar, or your cheese of choice
- Salt and Pepper to taste
- Pinch Cayenne Pepper

In a large stock pot over medium heat fry bacon pieces until nearly crisp. Remove quickly from pan, reserving grease for roux. Turn heat to low and add flour to grease, while stirring with a whisk. Whisk for about 2 minutes, allowing roux to cook slightly. Turn heat to high and *deglaze* pan with chicken stock. Add potatoes and simmer over medium heat until tender, stirring frequently.

Turn heat to low and add milk. Return the bacon to the pot, saving some for garnish. Cook for about 5 minutes without simmering. Add grated cheese and allow to melt. Season to taste. Garnish with bacon and a little bit of shredded cheese.

Roasted Garlic Tomato Soup

Serves 4-6

Nothing says quick comfort like a steamy bowl of tomato soup and a giant stack of grilled cheese sandwiches for dunking. Everyone has a preference as to how they eat their soup. My brother dunks the sandwich in—no spoon required. I save the sandwich for the very last, for sopping of course. More mannered individuals would probably drop the sandwich all together. However you eat it, here is my perfectly simple recipe for Tomato Soup with Roasted Garlic.

There are some that frown upon the use of anything canned. I however, see the practicality in a quality canned item.

2, 28 oz Cans Petite Diced Tomatoes, with Juice
2, 28 oz Cans Tomato Puree
3 Cloves Roasted Garlic, Crushed
1 ½ Tsp Kosher Salt
½ Tsp Pepper
Pinch Cayenne Pepper
½ Cup Heavy Cream

In a large stock pot, over medium heat, combine all cans of tomatoes, garlic cloves, salt, pepper and cayenne. Bring mixture to a simmer and allow to simmer for as long as your schedule allows. If I have the time, I keep it going for up to two hours. Thirty minutes of simmering should be the minimum. Stir frequently.

About ten minutes before serving, turn heat to low, and add cream. Be careful not to simmer this mixture. The acid in the tomatoes, along with the high heat, will curdle the cream. Taste and season accordingly.

CHAPTER 4: RECIPES

Cheddar Biscuits

Makes 8 biscuits

I try to serve bread with every dinner. This recipe for cheddar biscuits is a great variation to plain old bread and butter.

2 Cups Self Rising Flour
¼ Cup Vegetable Shortening
¾ Cup Cheddar Cheese, shredded
¼ Cup Green Onions, finely chopped
½ - ¾ Cup Buttermilk

> If you have some extra dough, and not enough biscuit eaters, refrigerate the leftover for dinner tomorrow. Simply spoon and bake before dinner.

Start by combining self-rising flour and vegetable shortening in a medium-sized mixing bowl. Work the shortening into the flour with your hands. Gather a handful of both shortening and flour between the palms of your hands and lightly sift the mixture back into the bowl. Repeat this step until the shortening is well incorporated. This can also be done by sifting the flour with one hand, as shown.

Next add the shredded cheddar cheese and chopped onions to the flour mixture. Toss with a wooden spoon to blend. Begin pouring buttermilk into the flour mixture, ½ cup at a time. Blend gently with a wooden spoon. If the dough looks dry, add the remaining buttermilk. Be careful not to over-mix the dough, or the biscuits will be tough. Stir only long enough for the flour to absorb the liquids.

Spoon biscuit dough onto a lightly greased sheet pan. Do so by filling a large spoon with about ¼ cup of dough, then scraping the dough onto the sheet with a smaller spoon. Space each biscuit about ½ inch apart.

Bake at 425 degrees for 10-15 minutes, watching carefully. The tops will be golden brown when the biscuits are done. Best served straight out of the oven.

CELEBRATING SIMPLICITY

Grilled Garlic Bread

The serving size depends on the size of the loaf you buy.

After tiring of the same old same old bread and butter for dinner, I started to grill slices of bread. The char marks makes for a nice contrast in flavors.

1 Loaf Italian Bread
¼ Cup Butter
1 Tsp Garlic, minced

> You can use any hearty bread in this recipe. We love focaccia, sour dough and ciabatta. If you have fresh herbs on hand, you can use those in the garlic butter, as well.

Slice the bread in 1 inch pieces. Melt butter with garlic in a small saucepan. Brush each piece, on both sides, with garlic butter.

On an outdoor grill, on medium heat, grill each side of the bread until grill marks appear. If you don't have a grill, you can use the broiler feature in your oven—just place buttered slices on a sheet pan, toast one side, then flip.

Roasted Chicken Pasta Salad

This salad serves 6-8 people and makes a great dish for a summer picnic or potluck!

6 Cups Cooked Penne Pasta

1 Cup Grape Tomatoes, quartered

1 Cup Sweet Corn

2 Cups Roasted Chicken, picked and cut into chunks

1 Cup Sour Cream

½ Cup Mayonnaise

2 Tbsp Cider Vinegar

2 Tbsp Sugar

Pinch Cayenne Pepper

Salt and Pepper to taste

Combine penne pasta, grape tomatoes and corn in a large mixing bowl. Use chicken picked from a roasted chicken, store bought, or one you have leftover! Cut into bite-sized cubes.

In another small mixing bowl blend sour cream, mayo, cider vinegar and sugar. Stir with a whisk. Season to taste with a pinch of cayenne pepper and a pinch of salt and pepper.

Pour dressing over the pasta mixture and gently toss until pasta is well coated. Chill for at least one hour before serving. This salad can be made up to two days before service.

> Save some time and cook the pasta ahead of time. Plan ahead and it can be refrigerated for up to 5 days in a sealed bag. Simply rinse the cooked pasta in cold water, then toss with 1 tablespoon of olive oil.

MAINS

Baked Rigatoni with Simple Meat Sauce

Serves 4-6…with leftovers!

I know that if I had an Italian Grandma, she would frown on this recipe. Unlike a traditional, homemade red sauce, this sauce can be made in under an hour! While most sauces are simmered for hours, this simple meat sauce has a fresh tomato flavor that will suit any palate. With only three main ingredients, the flavors (and grape tomatoes!) burst in your mouth.

1 lb Ground Beef

1 16 oz Can Petite Dice Tomatoes, with juice

1 Pt Grape Tomatoes, whole

Salt and Pepper to taste

2 Tsp Olive Oil

1 Tsp Balsamic Vinegar

4 Quarts Water

1 Tbsp Kosher Salt

½ lb Uncooked Rigatoni Pasta

1 Cup Mozzarella Cheese, grated

Cook ground beef over medium heat in a medium saucepan, or tall sided sauté pan. Drain grease, when meat is cooked. Stir in canned tomatoes and simmer over medium heat, uncovered, for a ½ an hour. Season to taste, add olive oil and vinegar.

While the sauce is simmering bring 4 quarts of water and kosher salt to a boil. Cook pasta according to package instructions. Drain pasta and rinse with cold water.

Toss pasta with sauce and place into a 9x13 baking dish. Top with grated cheese.

Bake pasta at 375 degrees for about 15 minutes, until the cheese is melted and the sauce is bubbly.

Meatloaf with Sweet Pepper Sauce

Serves 4

Meatloaf is a mainstay in nearly every family's dinner cycle. There are so many different versions, but this recipe is, in my neck of the woods, most like the original. The sweet pepper jelly is a subtle change; you can find this pepper jelly in the olive and condiment isle of your grocery store.

1 cup Ketchup

2 Tbsp Sweet Pepper Jelly

1 Tbsp Cider Vinegar

½ cup Brown Sugar

Kosher Salt and Fresh Ground Pepper to taste

½ Small Onion, chopped

1 tsp Olive Oil

1 lb Ground Beef

1 tsp Garlic, minced

2 tsp Worcestershire Sauce

1 egg

1 cup Bread Crumbs

In a small saucepan, combine ketchup, pepper jelly, vinegar and brown sugar. Simmer mixture on low for at least ½ an hour, stirring frequently. The sauce will darken in color and thicken slightly.

Sauté onions in a small sauté pan with olive oil on medium heat, until translucent. In a medium mixing bowl combine ground beef, sautéed onions, garlic, Worcestershire sauce, egg and bread crumbs.

CELEBRATING SIMPLICITY

Mix the meat ingredients with your hands, until well combined.

Press meat mixture into a greased medium sized baking dish. Be sure to press tightly so the meatloaf does not dry out and cooks evenly.

Bake meatloaf at 350 degrees for 15 minutes. After 15 minutes, spoon sauce over meatloaf and bake for another 5 minutes. Slice and serve.

One Pot Chicken Pie

Serves 4

2 Tbsp Butter

½ Cup Carrot, small dice

1 Cup Potatoes, peeled and diced

½ Cup Bell Pepper, small dice

1 Cup Zucchini, quartered and sliced

2 Cups Chicken Breasts, cubed

1 clove garlic, crushed

¾ Cup Flour

2 Cups Chicken Stock

Kosher Salt and Pepper to taste

1 Sheet Frozen Puff Pastry

1 Egg

In a medium-sized, oven-proof skillet, over medium heat, sauté carrots and potatoes in butter. Allow to cook for about 3 minutes.

Stir in diced peppers and zucchini. Sauté for another minute.

Stir in chicken and garlic and cook until chicken pieces are fully cooked.

Turn heat to low and stir in flour, cook on low for one minute then, deglaze pan with chicken stock.

Season mixture to taste. Allow to cool slightly. Place the sheet of puff pastry—it should be thawed but still cold for easy handling—on a floured surface. Cut dough to fit the top of your oven proof skillet. Place pastry dough over chicken mixture. If you have scrap dough and spare time, decorate the top of the dough.

Combine 1 egg with 2 tablespoons water, and brush over the top of puff pastry. Bake at 375 degrees until mixture is bubbly and top is browned, about 25 minutes.

Quick Broiled Chicken Wings

This recipe can serve anywhere from 2-6 people…depending on how serious they are about chicken wings!

Nothing says casual like a big platter of chicken wings. This recipe is so simple to prepare, and only requires a broiler in your oven to achieve perfectly crisp wings. The sauce is a slightly sweet, perfectly spicy, tomato based sauce. My only recommendation is — don't make these wings if you are on a first date or out to impress someone with your manners. They are messy!

BBQ Sauce

2 Cups Ketchup

½ Cup Brown Sugar

½ Cup Apple Cider Vinegar

2 Tbsp Worcestershire Sauce

2 Cloves Garlic

1 Tsp Salt

2 Tbsp Honey Mustard

¼ Tsp Chili Sauce

¼ Cup Honey

Wings

3 lbs Chicken Wings, trimmed and rinsed

3 Tbsp Olive Oil

1 ½ Tsp Kosher Salt

1 ½ Tsp Pepper

Combine all sauce ingredients in a medium-sized saucepan. Bring to a simmer over low to medium heat. Stirring frequently, simmer sauce for at least a ½ hour. This will take away the sharp flavor of the ketchup and result in a delightfully dark colored sauce.

Place wings in a large plastic bag, or large bowl. Coat with olive oil, salt and pepper and toss.

Line a sheet pan with foil then place a wire cooking rack onto the lined pan. Arrange wings on rack, fat side up, not touching.

CELEBRATING SIMPLICITY

Pre-heat broiler to high (about 500 degrees) and broil wings until browned on one side (about 10 minutes). Pull pan from oven and turn wings, cooked side down. Return to oven and broil until underside is crisp (about 5 minutes).

Pour warm barbeque sauce into a large mixing bowl. Transfer the cooked wings into the sauce and toss to coat. Serve immediately.

Simple Roasted Chicken

You can cut the chicken in 4-8 pieces, depending on how many you are serving.

1 Whole 4-5 lb Chicken
1 Tbsp Olive Oil
1 tsp Kosher Salt
1 tsp Ground Black Pepper

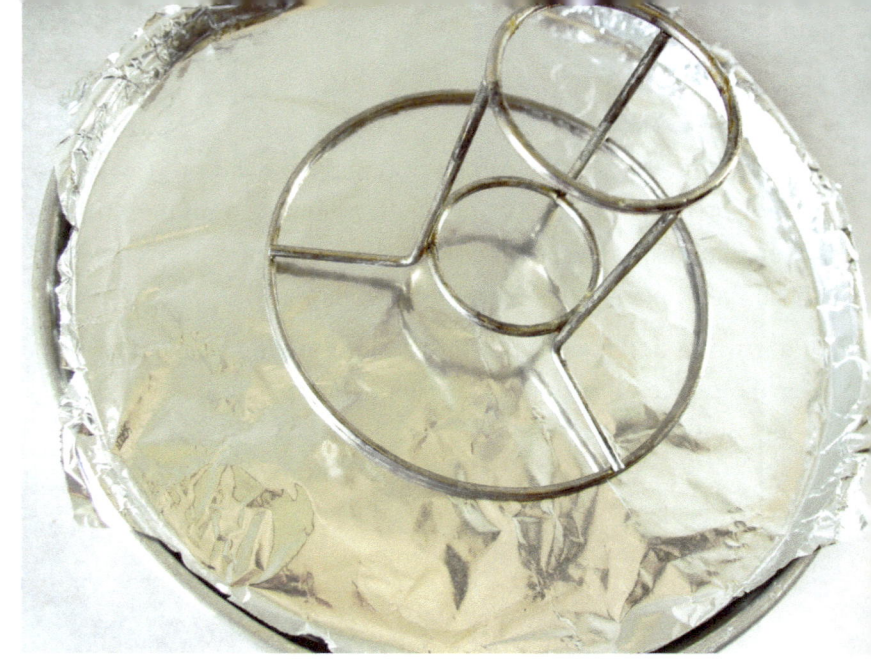

Place the chicken, bottom side down on a chicken rack. You can find a rack like this at most supermarkets, especially in the summer, since they are great for the grill. If you don't have a rack, simply sit the chicken on its bottom side. Place the chicken and rack on a small sheet pan, with sides, that is covered in aluminum foil.

Coat the entire outside of the chicken with oil, spreading with your hands. then sprinkle with salt and pepper.

Bake at 375 degrees for 40-50 minutes, until golden and internal temperature is 165 degrees. To measure temperature, insert the thermometer in the meatiest part of the thigh.

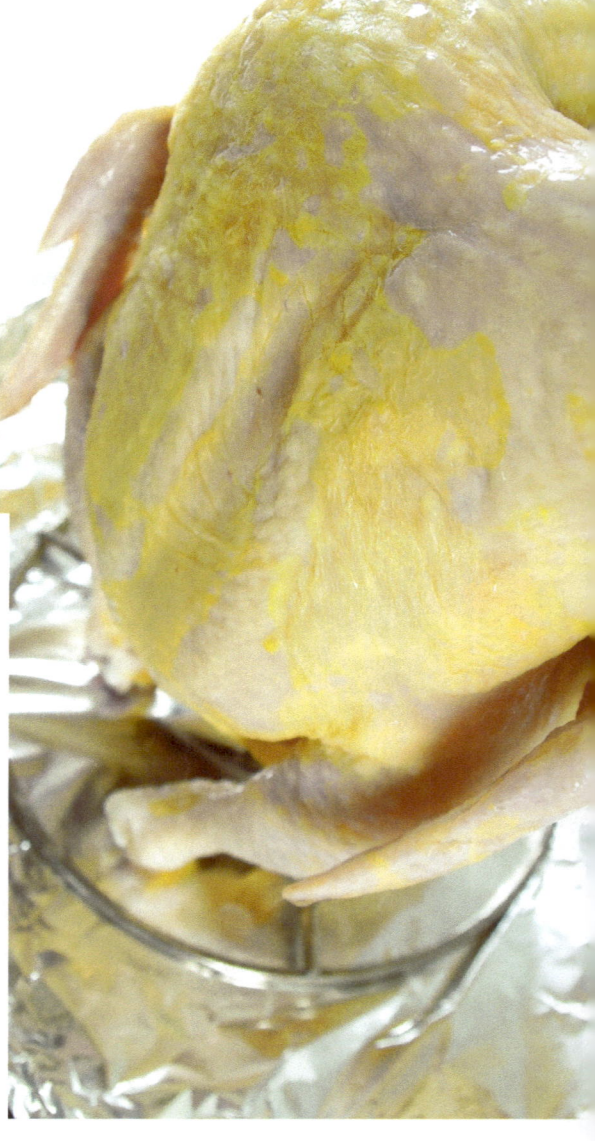

CELEBRATING SIMPLICITY

Let the cooked chicken stand for 5 minutes at room temperature. This will help the juices to absorb back into the meat, and not all over your cutting board. To cut the portions, lay the chicken on its back on a large cutting board. With a sharp boning knife, and a pair of tongs, remove each leg/thigh piece as shown.

Next, trim the wings by cutting at the end of the wing bone.

Slice the breast on one side (as shown) and follow along the rib cage of the chicken with your knife. This will remove the bones entirely from the breast piece, making it easier to eat. Serve immediately. Use the juices that from the bottom of the cooking pan to drizzle over the chicken.

Honey Lime Grilled Shrimp

Serves 4, 2 skewers per person

The mild flavor of shrimp lends itself well to marinades. This recipe is light and fresh tasting and is great on the grill. If you don't have a grill (or it's the middle of winter!) simply cook the shrimp in a sauté pan for 1 minute on each side.

½ Cup Olive Oil

3 Tbsp Honey

Juice of 1 Lime

¼ Tsp Red Pepper Flakes

Pinch of Salt

40 Shrimp, peeled with tails removed

8 Skewers

Soak the skewers, if they are made of wood, in a cup of water for at least ½ an hour. If the skewers are too long for the glass, flip them over halfway through soaking. This prevents the skewers from burning on the grill.

In a shallow dish combine oil, honey, lime juice, red pepper flakes and salt.

Place 5 pieces of shrimp on each skewer. When putting shrimp on the skewer, be sure to go through both the body and tail (as shown) so they are secure.

Place prepared skewers in the marinade and refrigerate for at least 1 hour. Flip the skewers half way through to soak both sides of the shrimp.

Preheat grill to medium heat. Place skewers on cleaned grill plates. Because of the oil in the marinade they will flame for a few seconds. Cook on each side for one minute. Raw shrimp is gray in color, and cooked shrimp will be light pink. Serve immediately.

CELEBRATING SIMPLICITY

Molasses Pork Tenderloin

Depending on the size of the tenderloins this recipe will serve 4-6 people. Sliced into ½ inch thick portions.

Pork tenderloin is by far one of my favorite cuts of pork—it's right up there with bacon! The flavor is great without a lot of seasoning or attention required. The molasses in the glaze is the perfect addition.

- 2 Pork Tenderloins
- 2 Tbsp Molasses
- 2 Tbsp Balsamic Vinegar
- 2 Tbsp Olive Oil
- ½ Tsp Kosher Salt
- ½ Tsp Ground Black Pepper

Trim loins by removing the ribbon, or silver skin. Peel back the ribbon with a sharp knife as shown; be careful not to cut into the meat. Place loins on a sheet pan lined with aluminum foil.

Combine molasses, vinegar and oil. Brush loins with molasses mixture.

Sprinkle with salt and pepper on all sides and roast at 375 degrees for 30 minutes. Remove from oven and let rest for 3 minutes. Slice then serve.

Pasta with Ham and Peas

I generally try to stay away from repeats in my weekly meals. I like to try new things, and raise the bar a bit each week. There are, however, a few recipes that slip through the cracks and can never be avoided. I love pasta with cream and peas. It is a flavor my family and I crave year round and eat often. The beauty of this recipe is that it is just as good with frozen peas as it is with fresh.

> A roux is a combination of equal parts fat to flour. You can use almost any fat, like butter, olive oil or even bacon grease. A roux is used in thickening dishes like sauces, soups and gravies.

- 8 oz Farfalle (bow tie) Pasta
- 4 Qt Water
- 1 Tbsp Kosher Salt
- 2 Tbsp Butter
- 2 Tbsp Flour
- 1 ¼ Cup Chicken Stock
- ½ Cup Frozen Peas
- ½ Cup Frozen Sweet Corn
- 1 Cup Chopped Ham
- ¼ Cup Parmesan Cheese, grated
- Pinch of Cayenne Pepper
- Salt and Pepper to taste
- ¼ Cup Heavy Cream

Bring 4 quarts water to a boil in a large covered stock pot. Remove lid, then cook pasta according to package instructions. Drain through colander and rinse with cold water. Set aside.

In a medium saute pan, over low heat, melt butter, then stir in flour. Cook while stirring for one minute. Pour in stock and turn heat to medium. Add peas and corn and simmer for about 4 minutes. Add ham and simmer for one more minute. Turn heat to low. Add cheese, cream, salt and pepper, and cayenne pepper then simmer for two minutes. Stir in cooked pasta and cook until heated. Garnish with freshly grated Parmesan cheese.

Simple Cheese Sauce

Makes: 1 gallon

This super easy cheese sauce is quick to prepare and can be used for almost anything you set your mind to. I use it with sharp cheddar cheese for my macaroni and cheese, with a good swiss cheese for a dipping sauce or some mozzarella for my Zucchini and Chicken Lasagna. {see page 62 for recipe}

¼ Cup Butter
¼ Cup Flour
2 Cups Chicken Stock
2 Cups Milk
2 Cups Cheese, grated
Kosher Salt
Fresh Cracked Pepper
Cayenne Pepper

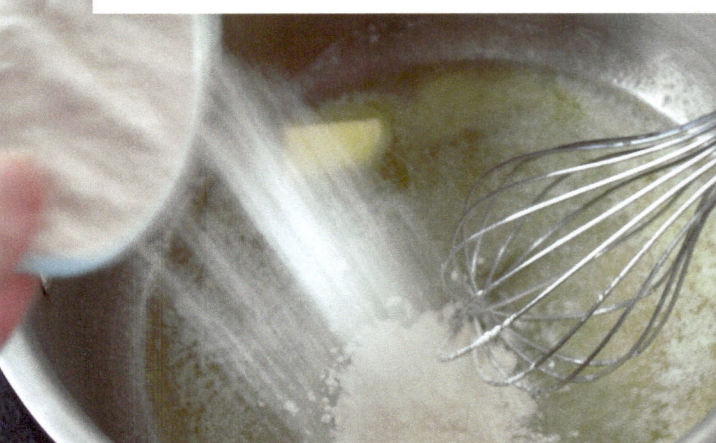

Begin by melting butter in a medium saucepan over low heat.

With a whisk, slowly stir in flour. While continuing to stir, cook the roux for about one minute.

Stir the chicken stock into the roux and simmer until thick bubbles appear—this shows your roux is working, and the sauce is thickening.

CELEBRATING SIMPLICITY

Next, stir in the milk and bring mixture back up to a simmer. Add cheese and allow to melt.

Once the cheese has melted, season with a pinch of kosher salt, black pepper and cayenne. When complete this cheese sauce can be used immediately in a recipe, or stored in the refrigerator for up to five days.

Zucchini and Chicken Lasagna

Serves 4

This recipe for lasagna substitutes the traditional ingredients with a white cheese sauce and chicken, making it a nice change for lasagna lovers! I like to make the lasagna in four individual dishes, but it can also be done in a medium baking dish, just follow layering instructions.

12 Lasagna Noodles
5 Quarts Water
1 Tbsp Kosher Salt
1 Tbsp Olive Oil

Filling

2 Tsp Olive Oil
1 Clove Garlic, chopped
1 Cup Red Bell Peppers, diced
1 ½ Cups Zucchini, quartered and diced
3 Cups Simple Cheese Sauce {see recipe 60 page}
3 Chicken Breasts
Parmesan Cheese
½ Cup Bread Crumbs

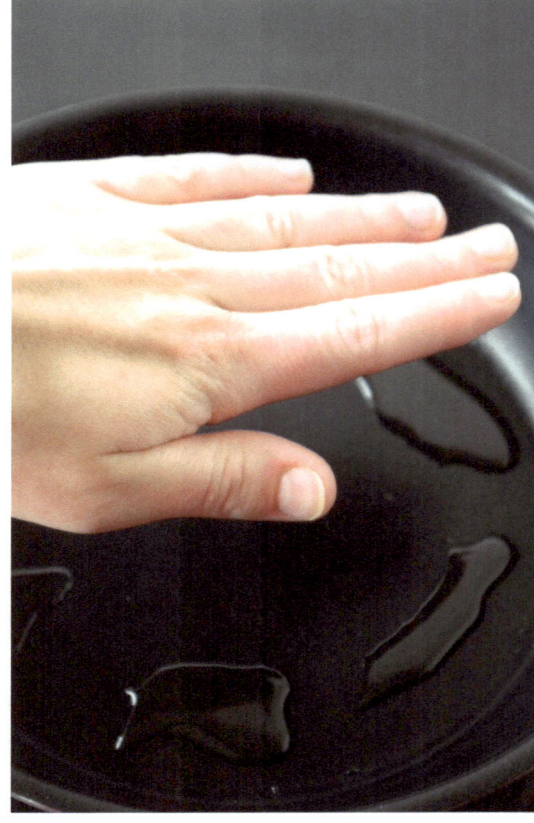

Bring water with kosher salt to a boil in a large covered stockpot over high heat. When boiling, remove lid and add noodles. Cook according to package instructions. Drain pasta through a colander, then rinse with cold water. Coat pasta with olive oil, and reserve until you are ready to assemble the lasagna.

Add 3 quarts of water to the same stock pot that you cooked the pasta in. Bring water to a boil and drop in chicken breasts. Cook until chicken is white all the way through. Remove from water and allow to cool. Once cooled, shred chicken into bite sized pieces with your hands.

In a small sauté pan over high heat, heat the oil. You can tell when the pan is hot enough to sauté by holding your hand, palm down, a few inches above the cooking surface. When the heat is too hot to hold your hand over, the pan is ready to cook.

Add chopped garlic, peppers and zucchini and sauté until nearly tender. Set mixture aside.

To layer the lasagna, place a small amount of cheese sauce in the bottom of each dish. Then place one noodle, split in half and overlapped on top.

Next, sprinkle sautéed vegetables and chicken over the noodles. Then pour a portion of the cheese sauce into each dish.

Repeat these layering steps until each dish has three layers of noodles. Sprinkle the top with breadcrumbs and grate parmesan cheese generously over each. Bake at 350 for 15-20 minutes, or until golden brown and bubbly.

SIDES

Herb Roasted Sweet Potatoes

Serves 4-6

Sweet potatoes are by far one of the most underused vegetables. In this recipe, the sweet potatoes are actually not sweet. Rather than smothering them in brown sugar and marshmallows, they are seasoned with herbs.

2 Medium Sweet Potatoes

2 Tbsp Chopped Fresh Herbs

2 Tbsp Olive Oil

½ Tsp Salt

You can use any fresh herb that you like in this recipe. I used oregano, but give basil, tarragon or parsley a try.

Peel the potatoes and cut into 1 inch cubes. Toss with chopped herbs, oil and salt. Place in one layer on a sheet pan. Bake at 425 degrees for 15-20 minutes or until golden and tender.

CELEBRATING SIMPLICITY

Pantry Potatoes

Serves 4

This recipe is by far one of the most frequently made recipes at my household! It is so simple to put together, and I always have the ingredients on hand. The Yukon gold potatoes are so flavorful that they don't need a lot of complex ingredients. You can also use red skin potatoes, or whatever you have available.

6-8 Medium Yukon Gold Potatoes

2 Tbsp Olive Oil

1 Tsp Kosher Salt

Fresh Ground Pepper

Clean and remove the eyes of the potatoes. Cut halfway vertically. Turn potatoes on the cut side and cut in quarters vertically.

CELEBRATING SIMPLICITY

Drizzle oil over wedges. Season with kosher salt and fresh ground pepper.

Place seasoned potatoes in a 13x9 inch pan. Bake at 400 degrees for 20-30 minutes or until potatoes are tender and golden.

Another great way to make these potatoes is with 2 Tablespoons of melted butter, instead of oil and ¼ cup of grated parmesan.

You can add crumbled bacon and cheddar cheese to this recipe to make it extra tasty!

CHAPTER 4: RECIPES

Roasted Asparagus

One bunch of Asparagus will serve 2-4 people. If you are cooking for a crowd simply buy a few more bunches.

This recipe is the perfect way to integrate some veggies into your dinner menu. It only takes 15 minutes to prepare, and is a definite crowd pleaser!

1 bunch Asparagus

1 Tbsp Olive Oil

1/4 tsp Kosher Salt

1/4 tsp Pepper

Rinse, then cut the asparagus about 3 inches up the stock. Discard the bottoms; the ends tend to be stringy and tough.

Line the asparagus on a sheet pan, in one layer. Drizzle with olive oil, season and coat.

Roast for 8-10 minutes at 375 degrees.

CELEBRATING SIMPLICITY

Home Style Cucumber Salad

Serves 4-6

There are certain vegetables that, when they come into season, you just can't get enough of them. Cucumbers, tomatoes, and sweet onions are just a few. When my family plants a garden, we always have plenty of these early summer veggies on hand. That is why we have some stand-by, go-to recipes that use all three. Our favorite recipe is this cucumber salad, which I adapted from a recipe given to us by a great country cook. This recipe is best after it chills for 2 or 3 days. You can also make it year round with veggies from the grocery store.

- 1 Cup Hot Water
- ¼ Cup Sugar
- ½ Tsp Kosher Salt
- 1 Cup Cider Vinegar
- 2 Tbsp Honey
- ½ Tsp Ground Pepper
- 2 Cups Seedless Cucumbers
- 1 Cup Roma Tomatoes
- ½ Cup Sweet Onion

In a medium-sized mixing bowl combine hot water, sugar and salt. Stir with a whisk until dissolved. Add cider vinegar, honey and ground pepper.

Wash and slice the cucumbers, discarding the end pieces.

One half of a medium onion will equal about a half of a cup. Slice the onion into thin slices. Remove the core of each tomato, then slice in half lengthwise. Cut into ½ inch slices. Add veggies to the dressing and toss to coat. Refrigerate before serving.

CHAPTER 4: RECIPES

Perfect Mashed Potatoes

Serves 4-6

Growing up in Amish country has set me on a quest to perfect the main staple of eating in my neck of the woods—Mashed Potatoes. I would say that some of my neighbors have this down pat and that is why I have taken most of my tips and techniques from them. You can make these with simple Idaho potatoes, or, if you're feeling fancy, use skin-on red potatoes.

6 Cups Potatoes

¾ Cup Milk

2 Tbsp Butter

1 Tbsp Sour Cream

Kosher Salt and Pepper to taste

Wash then peel the potatoes. Cut into 1 inch cubes.

Place cut potatoes in a medium stock pot and cover with water. Bring to a boil and boil until potatoes are tender. Drain water.

In the meantime simmer milk and butter in a small sauce pan over low heat, to warm. Warming the milk helps to keep the potatoes warm while you are mixing them—no one likes cold potatoes!

While in the same pot, beat cooked potatoes with a hand mixer until smooth. Adding additional ingredients before the potatoes are smooth will cause them to stay lumpy.

Turn mixer speed to low and slowly pour in warm milk and butter, then add sour cream. Blend well then season to taste.

CELEBRATING SIMPLICITY

Sautéed Green Beans with Brown Butter

Serves 4

This recipe for sautéed green beans is simple, yet has intense flavor. Simmering the beans in water helps to keep them perfectly al dente. You can use fresh or frozen green beans for this recipe—depending on the season.

- 2.5 lbs Fresh Green Beans
- 1 Cup Water
- 3 Tbsp Butter
- 1 Tsp Garlic, chopped

Wash beans, then remove both ends- be careful not to take off too much.

Place trimmed beans in a large sauté pan with ½ cup water. On high heat, simmer beans until water has evaporated. Add the remaining water and repeat.

In the meantime, melt butter in a small saucepan over low heat. Simmer butter until browned, then add garlic and remove from heat.

Pour browned butter over green beans and serve.

CHAPTER 4: RECIPES

DESERTS

Cranberry Crumb Bread

Makes 1 loaf

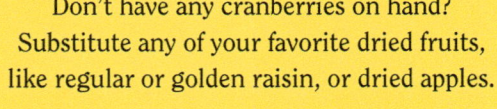
Don't have any cranberries on hand? Substitute any of your favorite dried fruits, like regular or golden raisin, or dried apples.

The best part about this bread is that it is quick and easy to make, and can be enjoyed any time of day! At breakfast, after dinner or as a wonderful gift to a friend.

Bread

2 Cups All Purpose Flour
½ Tsp Salt
1 ½ Tsp Baking Powder
1 Tsp Baking Soda
1 ½ Cup Sugar
3 Tbsp Butter, melted
½ Cup Sour Cream
½ Cup Milk
1 Tsp Vanilla
1 Cup Dried Cranberries, chopped

Topping

2 Tbsp Butter, melted
1 Cup All Purpose Flour
¼ Cup Sugar

In a large bowl, combine flour, salt, baking soda and powder. Add melted butter, sour cream, milk and vanilla. Beat with hand mixer on medium heat until well mixed. Stir in cranberries by hand, using a rubber spatula. Place batter in greased bread pan.

For the topping: In a small bowl, mix butter, flour and sugar with your hands. Mix until large crumbles form. Sprinkle topping over bread batter. Bake bread at 350 degrees for 40-50 minutes.

CELEBRATING SIMPLICITY

Fruit Cobbler

Serves 4-6

Whether you use fresh, frozen or canned fruit this cobbler recipe is so good. My Grandma uses canned fruit, but since I don't usually keep canned fruit on hand, I use frozen.

1 Stick Butter

1 Cup Self Rising Flour

1 Cup Sugar

1 Cup Milk

2 Cups Fruit

Melt one stick of butter and place in a 9x9 inch baking dish.

Add flour, sugar and milk- directly in the pan and whisk until well mixed.

Place fruit sporadically over the top of cobbler batter. You can use any of your favorite fruits like cherries, peaches, apples or blackberries.

Bake cobbler at 350 degrees for 50-60 minutes. The finished product should be golden brown on top. Serve warm plain or with some vanilla ice cream!

Vanilla Butter Cookies

Makes 1 ½ dozen

The best part about these cookies is that they are made with ingredients you should already have on hand. They are super quick to prepare! You can cut off as many cookies as you want, and refrigerate the rest of the dough for up to five days, and have cookies anytime.

1 ½ Sticks Butter, softened

¾ Cup Sugar

1 Egg

2 Cups Flour

½ Tsp Baking Soda

½ Tsp Baking Powder

½ Tsp Cream of Tartar

1 Tsp Vanilla

3 Tbsp Raw Sugar

Time Saving Tip:

Start the cookie dough before you start your dinner prep. Once you are done eating the dough will be chilled and ready to bake! Mmm… Warm Cookies!

Combine softened butter and sugar in a medium mixing bowl. Beat on high speed with a hand mixer, until fluffy (one minute). Add egg and beat for another minute. Add remaining ingredients (except raw sugar} and beat until the dough forms a ball. The texture will go from dry, to crumbly, to perfect in about 3 minutes.

Once dough is mixed, place it on a large sheet of plastic wrap. Form into a long tube, about 2 ½ inches wide.

Roll tightly in plastic wrap and secure the end. Refrigerate for at least ½ an hour.

CELEBRATING SIMPLICITY

When the dough has been chilled, slice into ¼ inch cookies while the dough is still cold.

Place raw sugar in a shallow bowl. Dip each cookie (top side down) into sugar, to coat lightly.

Arrange cookies about ½ inch apart on an un-greased sheet pan.

Bake at 350 degrees for 8-9 minutes. You do not want the cookies to turn brown; they will be too crisp. These cookies are best served warm, so bake what you need and get 'em while they're hot!

Quick Berry Cheesecake

Serves 4-6

Everyone loves a good cheesecake, but not everyone has the time to make their own. This recipe is simple and can be completed and ready to eat in just thirty minutes. I love to use fresh strawberries for this recipe, but you can use any berry, fresh or frozen.

Crust

1 Cup Graham Cracker Crumbs

¼ Cup Sugar

1 Tsp Cinnamon

2 Tbsp Butter, melted

Filling

8 oz Cream Cheese, at room temperature

1 Cup Heavy Whipping Cream

¼ Cup Sugar

¼ Tsp Lemon Juice

1 Tsp Vanilla

Topping

1 ½ Cups Berries

¼ Cup Sugar

Preheat oven to 350 degrees. In a small mixing bowl combine cracker crumbs, sugar and cinnamon. Transfer to an ungreased sheet pan and bake for ten minutes. This will toast the crumbs and blend the flavors of the sugar and cinnamon in well. Melt 2 tbsp of butter and mix into cooled crumb mixture. Set aside.

In a large mixing bowl, beat softened cream cheese with an electric hand mixer. Scrape the sides of the bowl with a spatula every now and then to ensure all of the cheese is being whipped. Mix for about two minutes on high speed. Scrape the sides of the bowl, then pour in heavy cream and turn speed to medium. Whip for another two minutes (mixer should be smooth and fluffy). Add sugar, lemon juice and vanilla and beat for one more minute. Set aside.

Prepare berries by washing and slicing them. Place sliced berries in a small bowl and toss with sugar. If you are using something like blackberries or blueberries, simply rinse them and toss in sugar, gently.

Begin layering by placing graham cracker crumbs in the bottom of a medium-sized, shallow serving dish. Next, spread cream cheese topping. Top with sugared berries and chill before serving. The berries tend to release a lot of juice when they are sliced. If there is a lot of liquid in your berry bowl, discard it and just spread the berries over your cheesecake.

Hosting a party? Prepare this recipe and present it in mini cupcake cups. Just follow the layering instructions with each cup and chill before serving. If you are making these a day in advance, put the strawberries on just before serving.

Peach Blueberry Crisp

Serves 4-6

Get your timer ready, because this throw together dessert is so quick and easy to make! I try to keep frozen fruit on hand for a last minute dessert fix. The great thing about this crisp is you can use many different fruits like cherries, apples or blackberries. Of course, they can be fresh or frozen, depending on the season.

2 Cups Peaches, sliced

1 Cup Blueberries

¾ Cup Sugar

2 Tbsp Flour

Dash Cinnamon

½ Cup Flour

½ Cup Brown Sugar

1 Cup Oatmeal

½ Stick Butter, softened

Combine peaches, blueberries, sugar, flour and cinnamon. Place in a medium sized baking dish.

In a medium sized mixing bowl blend together flour, brown sugar, oatmeal and softened butter- with your hands. Spread over top of peach mixture, bake at 350 degrees for 20- 25 minutes.

Apple Strudel

Serves 6-8

Apples, cinnamon and butter are welcome, comforting flavors any time of year. This recipe is a wonderful and different way to put those all together.

2 Sheets Frozen Puff Pastry
6-8 Apples, peeled and diced
1 Tbsp Butter
¾ Cup Brown Sugar
½ Tsp Cinnamon
½ Cup golden raisins
1 Egg

Allow puff pastry sheets to thaw at room temperature or in the refrigerator. Don't let the pastry sheets get too warm; it is easier to handle the pastry when it is cold. Peel and dice apples. Melt butter in a medium sauté pan and cook apples until nearly tender. Add brown sugar, cinnamon and raisins.

Place puff pastry on floured surface and roll out slightly. Spoon half of the apples onto the edge of the puff pastry, leaving about one inch excess of dough to fold when you roll the strudel. Mix egg with about 2 tablespoons of water, then brush around the edge of the dough. Roll the dough tightly around the apples, and fold in sides. Secure edge with egg wash, and brush top of strudel.

Bake at 375 degrees until golden, about 20-25 minutes.

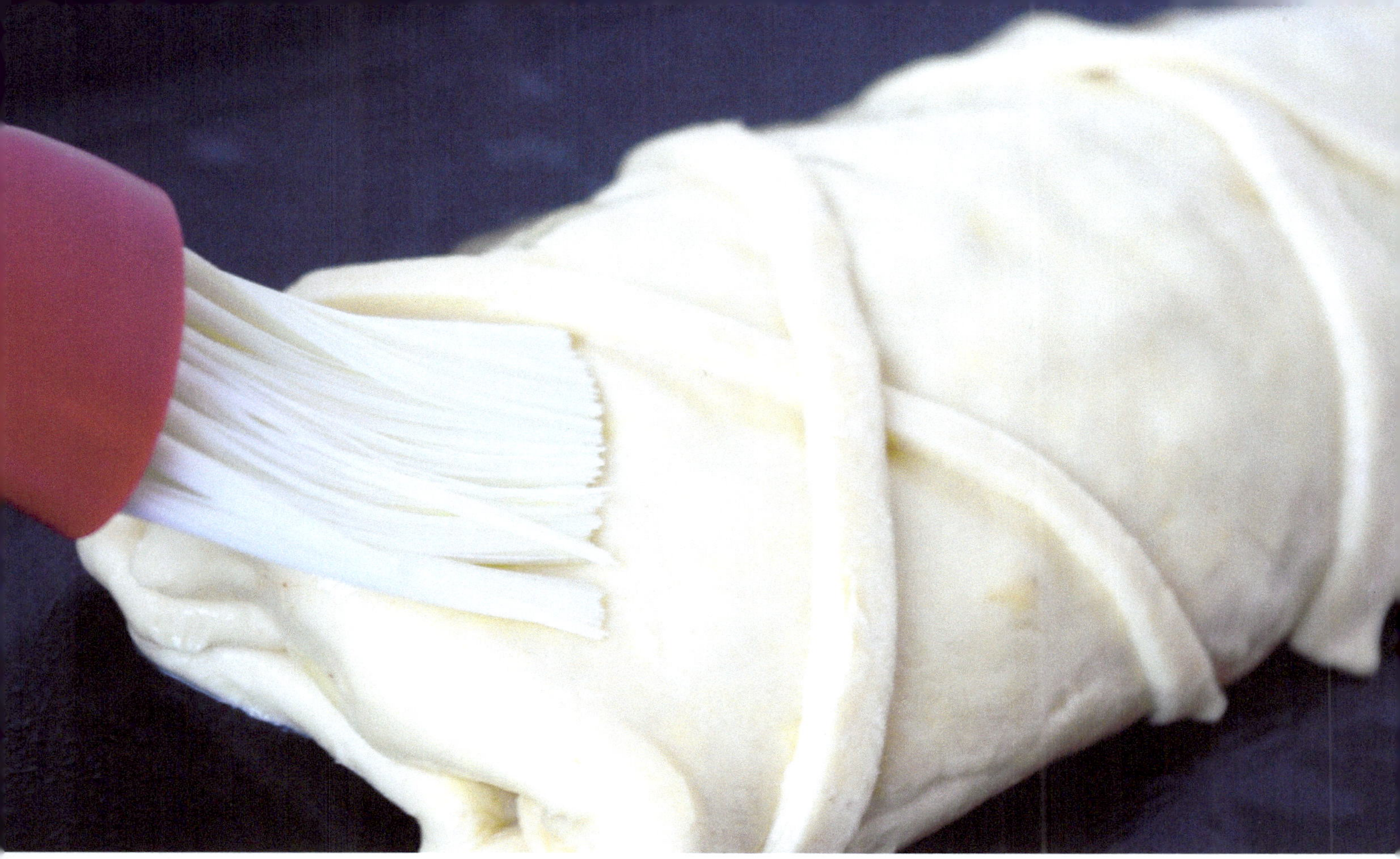

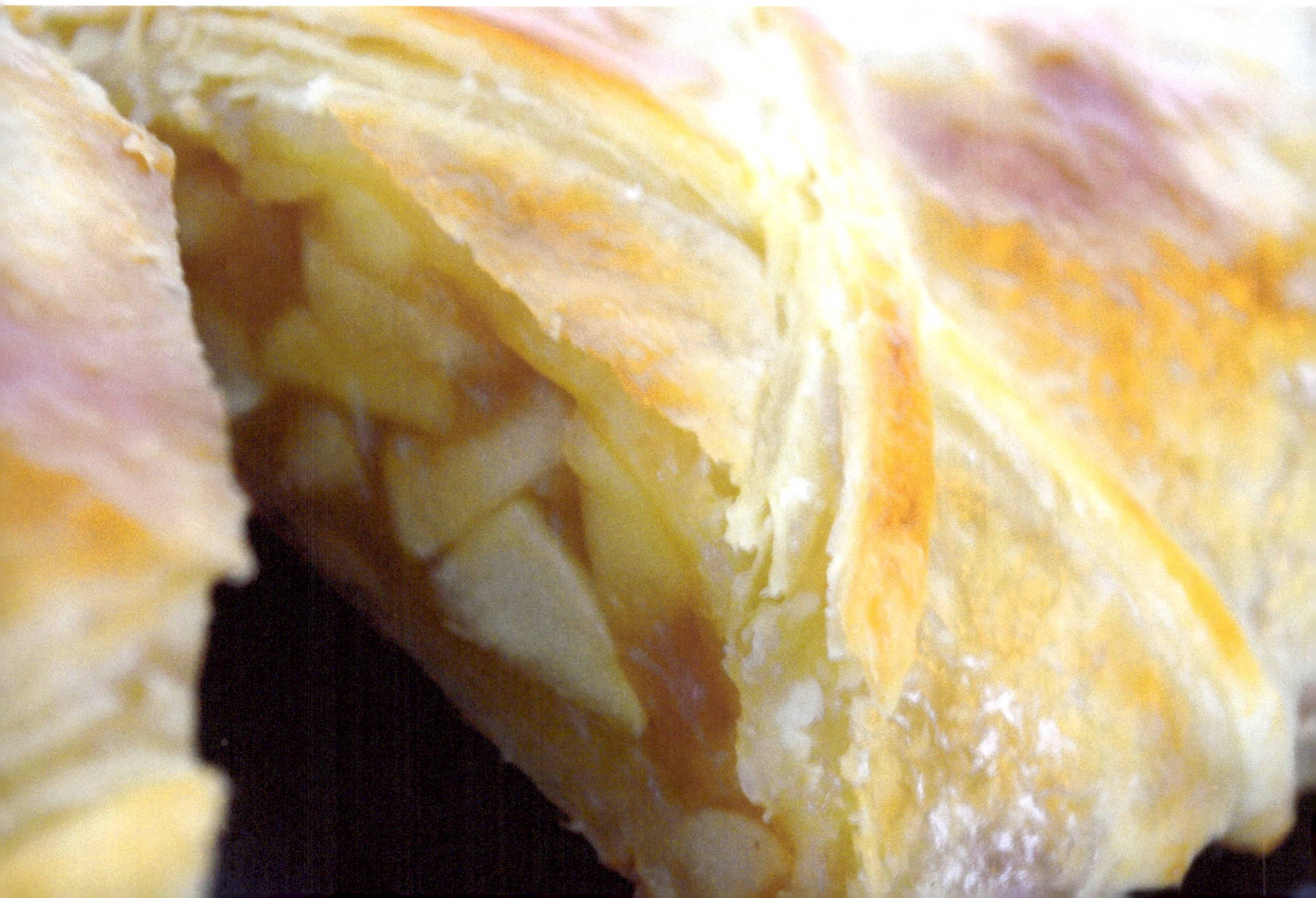

ABOUT THE AUTHOR
Stacey DeHass

STACEY DEHASS IS A CHEF FROM RURAL, OHIO. She is a Culinary graduate of the Wayne County Schools Career Center and Johnson & Wales University. After having the opportunity to learn and train under many great chefs, Stacey has now perfected her own cooking style—Simple and Approachable. She enjoys creating recipes and teaching home cooks all that they need to know to succeed. She has done so through cooking classes, seminars and now through her book, *Celebrating Simplicity*. For more information visit Stacey's websites: www.StaceyDeHass.com and for recipes www.StaceyCooks.com